D1021980

THE
GOOD FORTUNE
BIRTHDAY BOOK

This book belongs to

_____

_____

The gift of

_____

CHRONICLE BOOKS
SAN FRANCISCO

BIRTHSTONES AND MEANINGS

Month	Stone	Meaning
January	Garnet	Constancy
February	Amethyst	Sincerity
March	Bloodstone	Courage
April	Diamond	Innocence
May	Emerald	Success in Love
June	Pearl	Health
July	Ruby	Contented Mind
August	Sardonyx	Conjugal Felicity
September	Sapphire	Love
October	Opal	Hope
November	Topaz	Fidelity
December	Turquoise	Prosperity

FLOWERS

Month	Flower
January	Carnation
February	Violet
March	Jonquil
April	Sweet Pea
May	Lily of the Valley
June	Rose
July	Larkspur
August	Gladioli
September	Aster
October	Calendula
November	Chrysanthemum
December	Narcissus

WEDDING ANNIVERSARIES

1 _____	Paper
2 _____	Cotton
3 _____	Leather
4 _____	Fruit
5 _____	Wooden
6 _____	Sugar
7 _____	Woolen
8 _____	Pottery
9 _____	Willow
10 _____	Tin
11 _____	Steel
12 _____	Silk
13 _____	Lace
14 _____	Ivory
15 _____	Crystal
20 _____	China
25 _____	Silver
30 _____	Pearl
40 _____	Ruby
50 _____	Golden
75 _____	Diamond

JANUARY

BIRTHSTONE—Garnet: Constancy
FLOWER—Carnation
COLORS—Black and Dark Blue

January 1 to January 20 _____ Capricorn
Governed by Saturn
Mate in Libra, Virgo, or Taurus

January 21 to January 31 _____ Aquarius
Governed by Uranus
Mate in Aquarius

JANUARY 1

You are ambitious, studious, and original and have fine executive ability. You have self-respect and great personal charm. You are generous and affectionate and would make any sacrifice for your loved ones.

JANUARY 2

Your love of family is your strongest characteristic and your greatest charm. Your very devotion and earnestness to succeed for them will help you gain your success. With your generous and happy nature, you will win loyal, true, and devoted friends.

JANUARY 3

You are too apt to procrastinate and should practice diligence and perseverance, because you are capable of greater things. You are friendly and enjoy meeting new people, and you have a strong personality. The friends you make are lasting ones.

JANUARY 4

Yours is an energetic nature. You like to be doing things and seeing them well done. You have a faculty for making money, are shrewd, and have a good business ability. Those to whom you give your confidence will prove constant.

JANUARY 5

You are exceedingly honest, kind hearted, loving, and fond of children. You adapt yourself readily but should curb your tendency to criticize others. Your love is deep, and your home is dear to you.

JANUARY 6

You are impulsive; your actions are sometimes misunderstood and the motives misinterpreted. You think and act quickly and not always with good judgment. Cultivate poise and self-restraint, or your passions will lead you into serious difficulties even though your intentions are of the best.

JANUARY 7

Restrain your inclination to be exacting and domineering and learn to control your temper. You think a great deal of the opinion of others and strive to make a good impression. Marry young and choose a mate with sufficient character to stimulate your desire to be always at your best.

JANUARY 8

You are self-reliant, cautious, shrewd, dependable, and, being intuitive, can easily detect deception in others. You love music, art, and outdoor sports. You will always enjoy excellent health and should live to a ripe old age.

JANUARY 9

You have a frank, energetic, and progressive nature and have faith in the good performed by others. Those born on this day achieve their greatest success by adhering to the belief that they themselves are the masters of their success.

JANUARY 10

You are a natural leader and a good quick thinker. You would be successful in any commercial enterprise. Cultivate poise and do not be self-conscious or lacking in self-esteem. You attract the opposite sex and are unusually popular among your friends. Your love is true and loyal.

JANAURY 11

You are kind, loyal, and winsome, but secretive. Once you become a friend, it is for all time, but, in your fidelity, you are apt to overlook serious faults in these friendships. You will find success in business, politics, or teaching. You will make a happy and congenial marriage.

JANUARY 12

Your originality in everything you do, will, if cultivated, bring you happiness and remuneration. Your children will be mechanically inclined or artistic. You are naturally robust and strong, and, if you take care of yourself, you will never have any serious illness.

JANUARY 13

You are unusually energetic, independent, ambitious, and persevering. Unless they work for themselves, people of this nature gain nothing when tied to others. By gaining poise and control of your temper, you will be happier and more successful in your business and social life.

JANUARY 14

Never be satisfied with second best. Yours is the ability to do big things, and you are not easily discouraged. You have a sympathetic heart and concern yourself with the misfortunes of others. You are understanding and will make a loving parent, enjoy an ideal marriage, and have a happy home life.

JANUARY 15

You are very original, shrewd, and keen of mind. If you are a housewife, you are a good manager, a careful buyer, and diplomatic. If you go into business, it should be your own. You should curb your tendency toward brusqueness with subordinates and learn to encourage friendships.

JANUARY 16

You have courage, ambition, and singleness of purpose. You are sincere and just and should marry young. Do not try to analyze the motives and emotions of your love, and you will be sure of great happiness.

JANUARY 17

Through perseverance and adapting yourself, you will gain success. You are fair minded, just, and affectionate. You have great executive ability. Your true happiness will be found in a deep and trusting love.

JANUARY 18

You have a great deal of reserve power, which should be used more often to your better advantage. You are cautious, yet somewhat inclined toward suspicion. You want to love and be loved in return, but you seem unable to open your heart to your friends or your family.

JANUARY 19

Diplomats, writers, teachers, and lovers of the fine arts are born on this day. You have a kindly disposition, consideration, and a desire to help others. Poetical, artistic, and affectionate, you are capable of entering into almost any profession or field and being successful.

JANUARY 20

With more self-reliance, you are assured of success. Work honestly and diligently, and you will find happiness and pleasure in your work. March and November are the months in which you should begin important business. Tuesdays and Saturdays are your most favorable days.

JANUARY 21

You are adaptable, fond of good times, easygoing, and somewhat apt to take things for granted. You enjoy traveling and will do a great deal of it. Your tendency toward selfishness will bring you unhappiness in later life unless you learn to curb it.

JANUARY 22

You are self-reliant, diplomatic, and fond of dressing well, and you care a great deal for the good opinion of your friends and business associates. Though secretive, but not to the extent of trickery, you are affectionate and lovable and should make a happy circle wherever you are.

JANUARY 23

You are somewhat obstinate and difficult, and it is hard to drive you to do anything. Only those that know your weaknesses can rule you. You are well-liked and respected by everyone. You will live a happily married life.

JANUARY 24

Although you are good-natured, fair, and truthful, you are slightly inclined toward selfishness. You should marry early in life and choose a mate born in May, July, or November, and one spiritually inclined.

JANUARY 25

A born leader, you should strive to make the most of this gift. With your friendly nature, you will be surrounded with congenial friends and your home life will be a constant inspiration. Take care that anger and jealousy do not get the better of your otherwise good judgment.

JANUARY 26

Endowed with a great personal magnetism, you will always be surrounded by many people. Enjoy them! Your affections are not very deep, except to the one you will choose for your life partner. You are a true and loyal friend.

JANUARY 27

You have great ambitions and desires, and they will take you
far if you accept the help of others as you go along, instead
of trampling them underfoot. Accept love as it comes to you,
even when you think it retards your upward struggle.

JANUARY 28

Make the most of the talents you are blessed with, and ever
aspire to greater things. Be cautious and prudent; never
let your jealousy or envy of others come between you and
your happiness. Put your trust in those worthy of it. You are
sincere and you will win, through your sincerity, a deep and
true love.

JANUARY 29

You should take care in directing your natural ambition.
Follow one chosen profession or calling faithfully, and be
thorough and painstaking in whatever you undertake. You
are capable of loving deeply, and your marital and domestic
life will be ideal.

JANUARY 30

You are capable of exerting a great deal of influence over
those with whom you come in contact, and you should be
careful in using it. Develop your mind to the extent of its
capabilities. You are not demonstrative, but you can and will
love with a true, strong passion.

JANURY 31

You are ambitious, but you can be easily discouraged. You give up too easily where you might accomplish many things. You are kind, just, and generous and have an artistic temperament. Cultivate perseverance and confidence in your ability. You are fond of children.

MEMORANDA

FEBRUARY

BIRTHSTONE—Amethyst: Sincerity
FLOWER—Violet
COLORS—Light Blue and Yellow

February 1 to February 19 _____ Aquarius
    Governed by Uranus
    Mate in Aquarius

February 20 to February 29 _____ Pisces
    Governed by Jupiter
    Women mate in Cancer
    Men mate in Capricorn or Virgo

FEBRUARY 1

You have strong and definite emotions. You make a staunch and loyal friend, but a bitter enemy. You speak brusquely sometimes, without intention. You should learn to guard against jealousy. Take care that your desire for revenge does not spoil your happiness. You love your home and family life.

FEBRUARY 2

You have a strong personality and much charm and are capable of great good or evil. You like to dream too much and waste valuable time. You are an excellent conversationalist and enjoy culture and refinement. Your work should be active, and you will be very successful if you stick to it.

FEBRUARY 3

You should be married early in life to someone born in January, June, or October. You are kind, generous, and good-natured, and you have excellent self-control and keep your own counsel. You are fond of the out-of-doors and love pets and animals.

FEBRUARY 4

You are very frank and scrupulously honest in your business relations and your love. You are shrewd, have a strong personality, and command respect from all with whom you come in contact. You are fond of children and will have a happy home life.

FEBRUARY 5

You are a dreamer and inclined to be impractical. Follow through with your ideas and make each one be of merit! Choose your friends for their value, not their connections, or you will bring great unhappiness upon yourself. Be prudent rather than generous in your giving.

FEBRUARY 6

You have a keen sense of humor and are witty and fond of fun, though economical and prudent. You are inclined toward sensitiveness, which worries and annoys you. You should practice poise. You are demonstrative and loving, and you should have a very happy marriage.

FEBRUARY 7

Be self-confident and trusting, and you will enjoy your home and friends more. You have good judgment and a fine sense of character, but you should not let it predominate your friendships by constantly analyzing them.

FEBRUARY 8

It is easy for you to absorb a universal knowledge without much effort, because of your keen memory. You are very practical and not inclined to take things for granted in your home or business or in love. You are capable of a deep and lasting love, but you hesitate to accept others at their apparent worth.

FEBRUARY 9

Both the strongest and the weakest physically are born in this month. All have great possibilities, which, in some, attain high spiritual order. Study yourself and find your inclinations; then practice and apply yourself to them faithfully. You are loyal to your friends and constant in your love.

FEBRUARY 10

Practice self-reliance and concentration, and you will be successful, prosperous, and happy. You make and break engagements easily if they interfere with your convenience. You are energetic, kind, and affectionate, and your love will be constant.

FEBRUARY 11

Your laziness and indifference and your sometimes cynical
manner are drawbacks that you should try desperately to
overcome. You have latent talents that could be developed
to your advantage. You can be passionate and excitable, but
you usually are self-possessed and calm. In love you are not
indifferent.

FEBRUARY 12

Although you are a good and clear reasoner, you are, at
a critical time, apt to be impractical. Speculation would
be dangerous for you. You are fond of music and art and
have some ability with both. You prefer the company of the
opposite sex and are quite popular.

FEBRUARY 13

You have a happy and exuberant disposition and a consideration for the rights of others. You like refinement and culture, have good taste, are fond of good literature, and are ambitious to learn. In your love affairs, you do not like to stick to one person, but, after marriage, you will be very happy and contented.

FEBRUARY 14

One of your outstanding characteristics is independence. That is a virtue, but it should not be indulged to the point of selfishness. You enjoy praise when it is justly yours and dislike admitting error. You are masterful and very positive with men but indifferent toward women.

FEBRUARY 15

The satisfaction of your own whims and fancies is paramount in your life. You have talent and ability, but it will not show until some crisis brings it out. Although your interests are few, you thoroughly enjoy them, and your family is very dear to you.

FEBRUARY 16

You are a born leader, conscientious and careful in all you do. You are fond of art and the finer things of life and cherish integrity and honor. Your love is wholehearted and enduring, for which you will be rewarded.

FEBRUARY 17

You are fortunate to be born in this month. You have exceptional opportunities in love, business, or a career and can rise to the top. You are most considerate to those dear to you. You love with vigor, and your home life should be ideal.

FEBRUARY 18

Because you are blessed with determination, a methodical mind, and good executive ability, you will accomplish much and overcome many difficulties. You are careful, thrifty, and a good planner. You are a favorite among your friends and associates.

FEBRUARY 19

You are conscientious and reliable and plod along in your work faithfully. You like travel and a change of scene. You are honest and wholehearted in your love, and it will bring joy and contentment to you.

FEBRUARY 20

Your passions are deep, and you love and hate with intensity. You lose control of your emotions easily and act hastily when excited, but you quickly regain your better judgment and make amends. You have a great deal of personal pride and like to command.

FEBRUARY 21

You have excellent reasoning powers but are somewhat critical in your opinions. You are studious, serious, and self-contained, enjoy reading good literature, and like the finer things in life. You will have a pleasant and happy home life.

FEBRUARY 22

Cultivate self-confidence, self-esteem, and a better outlook on life; you are too apt to be pessimistic. You are capable of great things if you will accept the present happiness and not worry about the future. You are generous to a fault and can love deeply.

FEBRUARY 23

You will always enjoy good health and prosperity. You are farsighted, determined, and well balanced. Just and loving, you are generally well liked by all your friends and associates. Your home is very dear to you.

FEBRUARY 24

You are sweet tempered, kindly, acquiescent, and retiring. You should choose a mate that is of strong character and robust to complement your quiet temperament. You enjoy serenity and like to be surrounded with luxury.

FEBRUARY 25

You have a gift of quick and very keen perception, which you should use intelligently and to the greatest advantage. You have a very vivid memory. Your first impressions of people are best. You are impulsive and will marry after a brief courtship.

FEBRUARY 26

When you can forget yourself, you are very entertaining. You are intellectual but inclined to be oversensitive and should cultivate self-confidence. You are careful and considerate, and, although slow in drawing conclusions, you are unusually accurate in your judgment. You are affectionate and loving.

FEBRUARY 27

You have an acquisitive faculty that, if cultivated, will make you very successful. You are restless but methodical in your habits and fond of responsibility, and you like to be a leader. You are devoted to your family and have their love and respect.

FEBRUARY 28

You are spiritually inclined and your interest in religion is absorbing, but your analytical mind will not let you accept any doctrine or follow any sect without understanding it. You are loving and sincere and fond of travel and outdoor sports.

FEBRUARY 29

You are gentle and sympathetic and considerate of others, and you are easily influenced, and like a change of environment. Your love of literature colors your conversation so that you are in great social demand. You can readily adapt yourself to circumstances. You like attention, and your love is true.

MEMORANDA

MARCH

BIRTHSTONE—Bloodstone: Courage
FLOWER—Jonquil
COLOR—White

March 1 to March 21 _____ Pisces
Governed by Jupiter
Women mate in Cancer
Men mate in Capricorn or Virgo

March 22 to March 31 _____ Aries
Governed by Mars
Mate in Leo or Sagittarius

MARCH 1

You have definite artistic tendencies, which should be developed to your good advantage. You have faith in yourself and your ability and will be successful. You are honest, frank, good-natured, and sincere in your affections. You will win a deep and lasting love.

MARCH 2

Practice sincerity, patience, and diligence in your ambitions and everyday life. Be less skeptical. You have great self-control and psychic powers and are an excellent conversationalist. You have many friends and prefer the company of the opposite sex but are well liked by your own.

MARCH 3

You have a magnetic personality, and you should take care that this gift does not lead you into difficulties. You are passionate and your emotions sometimes overpower you, but your love, though fervent, is constant. You like and appreciate music and have some musical ability.

MARCH 4

Your personality is winning and gracious but somewhat given to criticizing. You are easily influenced, and you should try to be bold, diligent, and faithful. You are a shrewd judge of people and are generally right in your estimate. You are fond of children.

MARCH 5

You have the gift of farsightedness and are a good planner. All important undertakings should be begun during May and June. You are a true and loyal friend and an ardent lover. You will always be contented and happy.

MARCH 6

Don't marry hastily! With your temperament, an uncongenial mate would make your married life very unhappy. You have a strong will and are self-reliant and inclined to analyze everything. You are fond of sports and excitement. You enjoy having lots of people around you and like making new acquaintances.

MARCH 7

You should be more forward; assert yourself. You are slow, methodical, and extremely careful in all you do. Because of your cautious temperament, you are apt not to go through with plans you make. You are generous to a fault and very tenderhearted, and, too often, you allow others to impose upon you.

MARCH 8

With your keen appreciation of good literature and music, you would make a good critic of both. Although you are frank, straightforward, and scrupulously honest, you like personal attention and are apt to seek it. Your love is steadfast and your friendships lasting.

MARCH 9

Although you are spiritually inclined, you enjoy outside interests of the higher type. Your home life is very dear to you. You are careful and a good planner, and, as a real leader, you have the faculty of being able to interest others in the things that interest you. You would make a devoted parent.

MARCH 10

With a quick perception and a keen understanding of human nature, you are led by suggestion rather than force. The love and friendships you inspire are true and lasting, and you have no real enemies. You are observing and like to travel, and you will do so extensively.

MARCH 11

In adversity, you are spurred on, rather than discouraged. You are an ardent lover and the bitterest enemy. Never halfway in your work or social life, you are enthusiastic in whatever you undertake.

MARCH 12

You have a friendly and engaging personality, and you form many lasting friendships. You should let your gift of intuition guide you, as it is more accurate than your carefully drawn conclusions. You are impulsive in love but honest and faithful.

MARCH 13

Let the success of your many ambitions make you happy, and forget past failures. Study yourself and develop all your latent talents. You make friends easily and have many loyal and true ones.

MARCH 14

You are fond of society and a good conversationalist, and your company is sought by all. You are energetic and a clear thinker. With your blessed combination of ambition and friendly disposition, you should achieve great success in anything you undertake.

MARCH 15

Modest and unassuming, you nevertheless have a strong personality that enables you to take a leading part in all you do. You have the entire confidence of your friends and associates, and your love is wholehearted and sincere.

MARCH 16

Your serious nature is known by only your most intimate friends, because you cover it with a blithe and happy-go-lucky disposition. Any unhappiness is kept to yourself, and you are kind without the knowledge of others. You can command a great love and will be very happy.

MARCH 17

You are retiring, thoughtful, and rather philosophical, and you have definite opinions. You do not invite the advances of others, and, when you receive them, you are indifferent. Those who are fortunate enough to gain your confidence are true and loyal friends.

MARCH 18

Cultivate your self-confidence and be less restless and anxious; you have ability. You love your home life, and your circle of friends, though small, are a strong force in your life. You will always be happy.

MARCH 19

You are domestic, kind, extremely generous, gentle, and sensitive. If you are not in harmonious surroundings, you are completely miserable. You need an unusual amount of love and understanding. Your sweet and adoring disposition will undoubtedly or probably win this affection.

MARCH 20

You are studious, intellectual, and a logical thinker. You are fond of travel and gaiety, and your retrospective tendency makes your pleasures and observations permanent. You will love deeply, work diligently, and play with childlike abandon.

MARCH 21

You are impetuous, persistent, and somewhat stubborn. You are kind and loving in your marital relations, and, if you cause any unhappiness by your impatience, you are quick to make amends. You are a leader, and are sincere in all things and with all people.

MARCH 22

You have a very friendly disposition and are liked by everyone. You are happy and fond of pleasure, but, when working, you concentrate all your efforts and turn out a job well done. You are sincere and generous in your love.

MARCH 23

A good executive and meticulous about detail, you are a born leader in business and in your social life. You are considerate of others and friendly. You will have a happy married life with many children.

MARCH 24

You are naturally industrious and self-sufficient. For those you love, you will exert all your energies toward making them happy. You are very affectionate, especially intuitive, somewhat psychic, and never enthusiastic.

MARCH 25

Through your openhearted, generous nature, you will make many real friends and a happy marriage. You are careful and thrifty, and you will follow the plans you make for your future with care and precision to a successful conclusion.

MARCH 26

You are very positive in your opinions and dislike opposition, which is apt to make you bitter. You are generous, but you will not allow imposition. You do not invite advances and are rather shy, but, when you do yield, you will love with a deep, overpowering passion.

MARCH 27

Originality, courage, and a keen sense of humor are your chief characteristics. You love good times and like to share them. You are naturally friendly and enjoy a large circle of friends.

MARCH 28

Positive and aggressive, you enjoy having people around you. The men born on this day are fortunate and successful in business. The women are good housekeepers, insofar as management of the household and family affairs are concerned, but actual housework is distasteful to them.

MARCH 29

You are affectionate and love with wholeheartedness and sincerity, but you should not let your heart rule your head. You are sensitive and romantic. Cultivate more self-confidence; you have great ability and could be a leader if you had greater self-esteem.

MARCH 30

You are analytical and give a great deal of thought and careful consideration to a problem before doing anything important. Be less skeptical in your opinion of others. You are loving and will have a happy home life.

MARCH 31

You are intellectual, kindhearted, and loving. You enjoy music and have quite an artistic temperament. Women born on this day make devoted wives and excellent mothers and are the very nucleus of the home.

MEMORANDA

APRIL

BIRTHSTONE—Diamond: Innocence
FLOWER—Sweet Pea
COLORS—Yellow and Red

April 1 to April 20 _____ Aries
    Governed by Mars
    Mate in Leo or Sagittarius

April 21 to April 30 _____ Taurus
    Governed by Venus
    Mate in Virgo, Capricorn, or Libra

APRIL 1

You are a fairly good planner but not a very good executive. As the power behind the throne, you can direct others better than doing it yourself. Your ambitions are high and you make great sacrifices to attain them. You will have a happy home life, and love will play a great part in your life.

APRIL 2

With your extremely generous nature, you are imposed upon by others. You are sociable and gracious and have a pleasing personality. You enjoy outdoor life and are especially fond of flowers. You family is very dear to you, and you will always have many friends.

APRIL 3

You should marry young, preferably to someone born in December. The habits you form and the social contacts you make in your early life will stay with you in your late life. You do not possess much adaptability. You are slow and deliberate, but these qualities will bring you success.

APRIL 4

You are very ambitious and apt to overdo your zeal for success. Do not let disappointments or failures dishearten you. You are resourceful and able to do many things. You are capable of a deep love.

APRIL 5

You have been endowed with strength and fortitude. Cultivate these qualities! You have a magnetic personality and the qualities of a good leader. Your home life is dear to you, and you are fortunate in having a large circle of friends.

APRIL 6

You read a great deal and enjoy good literature. You are a good conversationalist but do not care for light talk. You are rather domestic and live very much within yourself. You are well liked, for you are interesting and entertaining.

APRIL 7

You are an enthusiastic planner, and you carry out your plans in the easiest way rather than to a glorious finish. You love social life and enjoy entertaining. Your love is ardent and enduring.

APRIL 8

You are punctual, and, when you start things, you like to see them move rapidly to completion. You are somewhat impatient, impulsive, and argumentative. You have many true and steadfast friends.

APRIL 9

Your outstanding characteristics are honesty, dependability, integrity, and an indomitable ambition. Your advice is often sought to the advantage of the recipient. You are a staunch, loyal friend and have deep affection and respect for your home ties.

APRIL 10

You are fastidious in your ideas and careful of appearances at all times. You are both artistic and idealistic. You think quickly but act slowly. You are tender, kind, and considerate, you love deeply, and you have the sincere love of your kin and your immediate household.

APRIL 11

You can adapt yourself readily to a change of environment, and you are faithful to duty, loyal to your friends, and enthusiastic in your work. You have great power of determination, and, through it, you successfully surmount many difficulties. Your love is deep, and you will compel the same in return.

APRIL 12

You are naturally very cautious and act only after due consideration. Your decision made, you will not retract any part of it and will carry all responsibility. You love your home and continually try to make it more pleasant and attractive.

APRIL 13

You have perseverance and are energetic and versatile. You are easygoing, and, when thwarted in your purpose, you are resourceful in accomplishing it in other ways. You are quiet, reserved, and uncommunicative and do not make friends easily, but you hold the few you make. Your love is sincere and steadfast.

APRIL 14

You have a strong, keen mind, a gentle and kindly disposition, and a good intuitive judgment. You have good and practical ideas. Your love is generous and sometimes extravagant. Your mate should be one of like interests, and your happiness is assured.

APRIL 15

You are very courageous and have keen perception and an analytical mind. You like society, travel, and popularity and you are led by your ambitions. You do not let unpleasant surroundings disturb you. You are an ardent lover.

APRIL 16

You are ambitious and plan many things, which you usually carry out. You are energetic and enthusiastic, and, though you graciously listen to others' advice or criticism, you pursue your own course. You are loving and will have a happy home life.

APRIL 17

You are an ardent reader and strive to improve yourself generally. You are sensitive and, when happy, are extremely exuberant, and, when unhappy, are depressed. You are affectionate and require a deep and understanding love, which you will reciprocate.

APRIL 18

You possess a sunny disposition and are moderately patient, loving, and sincere. You are ambitious and strive to do the unusual. Do not let the imposing size of your enterprise deter you. You have intellectual ability and physical strength to help and guide you.

APRIL 19

You have an artistic temperament and are intellectual and fond of music and travel. You enjoy outdoor sports. You should take great pride in your possessions and abilities and use them to your best advantage. You are sincere and will have many close friendships.

APRIL 20

Your positive and headstrong ways will carry you over many obstacles to success. You expect others to step aside or be trampled on. You are influenced by praise and flattery, rather than by direct appeal or command. You have your family's respect and devotion.

APRIL 21

You are kindhearted, generous, ambitious, and easily influenced by the opinion of others. You enjoy culture and refinement and should find success and happiness in the fine arts. You should take great care in selecting your life partner; a mate who does not have the same interests will bring you unhappiness.

APRIL 22

You have a musical talent, which should be developed. You are positive in your opinions, but, when thoroughly convinced, you yield with good grace. You have a clear and alert mind and keen foresight. You are capable of a deep and sacrificing love.

APRIL 23

You like and desire fine surroundings and are unhappy without them. You are strong willed and dominating, and you like to lead and expect complete obedience from your subordinates. Your love is masterful and passionate.

APRIL 24

You read a great deal and retain and absorb the knowledge gleaned from it to use in your conversation. You seek the society of other well-read and cultured people and scorn superficial study. You like personal attention but dislike flattery.

APRIL 25

You are clever and skillful with your hands. Your love is ardent and irresistible. You are frank and outspoken without being malicious. You possess jealousy and demand undivided love and attention.

APRIL 26

You are shrewd, farsighted, and ambitious. Your friends and associates have confidence in you and respect you. Your most valuable possessions are your friends, who are staunch and loyal and will help you when in need. You love your home life and are kind and considerate of your family.

APRIL 27

You are sometimes stubborn but not quarrelsome. You are fair with people and expect fairness in return. You are strong willed and your head very definitely rules your heart. You are a leader in any group you are a part of.

APRIL 28

You live within yourself. Rather than make any of those you love unhappy, you keep your troubles and worries to yourself. You have determination of purpose and always do what you plan. You are sincere and straightforward in all things.

APRIL 29

You are cautious yet shrewd, positive, and intuitive, but sometimes people take advantage of you in spite of these qualities. You always want to act on your intuition, but your cautious nature holds you back, causing a constant dispute within you. You are sensitive and easily offended.

APRIL 30

You are frank and very outspoken and sometimes unintentionally hurt others' feelings. You are faithful, dependable, and conscientious. To those you love, you are devoted and have their deep and sincere affection.

MAY

BIRTHSTONE—Emerald: Success in Love
FLOWER—Lily of the Valley
COLORS—Yellow and Red

May 1 to May 21 _____Taurus
    Governed by Venus
    Mate in Virgo, Capricorn, or Libra

May 22 to May 31 _____ Gemini
    Governed by Mercury
    Mate in Libra, Aquarius, or Gemini

MAY 1

You are strong willed, energetic, impulsive, a good planner with a fine executive ability. You are blessed with a vivid personality. You love intensely. In love, your path has its ups and downs, but you will find a great happiness.

MAY 2

You are patient and kind, and you like pleasant surroundings, but you are uncommunicative and keep your troubles to yourself. Everyone likes you, and you have no enemies. You will make a devoted and understanding parent.

MAY 3

You are punctilious and exacting and expect the same in others. You are shrewd, calculating, and cautious, never entering into any undertaking until it has been thoroughly considered. Your family is devoted to you, and you could be happier in your home if you would let yourself.

MAY 4

You are witty, original, intelligent, and always doing the unexpected. You are friendly and are very popular. You can adapt yourself to circumstances or environment and are loving and fond of children.

MAY 5

You are imaginative, almost visionary. You take pride in being well dressed. You like flattery and enjoy society. Responsibility does not mean much to you. However, you are a charming person and pleasant to live with and should have a happy home life.

MAY 6

You are proud, persevering, conscientious, and sometimes stubborn. You are constantly striving to elevate yourself socially and intellectually. You have a tendency toward pessimism that with continued unhappiness or failure might cause you to become bitter and caustic. You are usually kind and tender.

MAY 7

You are a slow and plodding worker. You are shrewd and clear-sighted, and your judgment is very good. You have much self-esteem, ambition, and ability. You are capable of a strong and devoted love and will have a pleasant home life.

MAY 8

You have a sunny disposition and a charming personality and quite a bit of originality, wit, and humor. Have more self-confidence in your abilities. You like light literature and good times. You will always be happy.

MAY 9

You have originality and should cultivate your creative
ability. You are amusing and entertaining, and you are
popular among your friends and associates and have
definite likes and dislikes. You should marry young; your
home life will bring you much happiness.

MAY 10

You are persistent, mentally alert, and levelheaded, and you
never let failure or adversity deter your effort or lessen your
spirit. You are courteous, diplomatic, and gracious, never
showing your true feelings unless they are pleasant.

MAY 11

Strong, both mentally and physically, you are versatile, energetic, and artistic. You enjoy reading very much. You are good-natured, happy in your home life, popular, and accepted as a pleasant and reliable person. You would be successful in an executive position.

MAY 12

You are a clear thinker and logical in your reasoning. You are ambitious to learn and better yourself. You enjoy good literature and music and like artistic surroundings. You need an unusual amount of love and understanding and are demonstrative in your love.

MAY 13

You are honest, sincere, intellectual, and rather retiring, and, though you are moody sometimes, you are kind and lovable most of the time. You like traveling because of the educational value, and you make the most of your opportunities to better yourself.

MAY 14

You can attain any goal you really set your heart on. You are determined, independent, dominating, and sometimes inclined to be headstrong. Your mind is clear and alert, and it absorbs and retains what you see and hear. You are sincere and generous in your love. You are a loyal friend and a bitter enemy.

MAY 15

You have great ability and natural aptitude. You are a constant reader and enjoy only good literature. Observant, critical, shrewd, and cautious, you are a competent social leader. You are a loving parent and the direct source of all happiness in your home.

MAY 16

You are a clear thinker and have an excellent memory and good ideas and the ability to carry them out. You have a keen sense of humor and a sincere and deep love for your home, which is all-important to you.

MAY 17

With your pleasant and genial disposition, you are clever,
intellectual, and discriminating. You like good times and
the social whirl. You are more popular with the opposite sex
than with your own.

MAY 18

You are too fond of taking a chance and should curb this
tendency, as it will bring you unhappiness and restlessness.
You waste precious efforts and energy in following that
desire. You enjoy music and art and like children, and your
home is very dear to you.

MAY 19

You are nervous, energetic, and somewhat excitable. You play with childlike abandon and seek gaiety. You are kind, considerate, and affectionate in your love. You are witty and fond of fun.

MAY 20

To be perfectly happy, you require a deep and strong love. You are serious in your thinking, your actions, and your love. Reading is your favorite pastime, and you are blessed with an assimilative memory.

MAY 21

You have a great deal of confidence in your ability and what you can accomplish. You are original and compelling, and you enjoy nature and sports. You love your home, like to make it beautiful, and are devoted to your family.

MAY 22

The abundant ability and talent you possess will not be evident until some crisis or need arouses it. You have a great deal of pride; do not let it rule you. You are gentle, kind, and sincere and should marry someone who has the same interests and will bring out the best in you.

MAY 23

You are enthusiastic in everything, work or play, and will try anything. Failure or adversity cannot discourage you. You have self-esteem, assurance, and a persistent determination. You are fond of art, literature, and music and are vivacious and witty. Happiness is assured you.

MAY 24

You give unlimited concentration and enthusiasm to your work. With your magnetic personality and strong character, you are a leader. Sincere and trustworthy, you love as intensely as you work.

MAY 25

You put sincerity and your best efforts into any undertaking,
but sometimes your ideas are impractical and fantastic.
You should keep your passions and emotions under strong
control. You are capable of loving deeply, and you require
affection in return.

MAY 26

You are lighthearted, exuberant, and fond of gaiety. You
like having people around, you like to please them, and are
enthusiastic over new friends. Sometimes passionate and
excitable, you are friendly, irresistible, and lovable.

MAY 27

You are a loyal and steadfast friend, and you hold your friendships. You are exacting, you like your own way, and you are very determined in your efforts to get it. Witty, sociable, and an interesting conversationalist, you attract others to the home you love.

MAY 28

You are ambitious, self-satisfied, and determined, but sometimes stubborn. You like social life, especially in a circle above your own, and can readily adapt yourself to it. Your home is very dear to you; you constantly make sacrifices and spare no expense to make it better and happier.

MAY 29

You are domestic, fond of children, affable, and considerate. You love your family and are very affectionate toward them. You have a sweet, even disposition, but you are aroused to bitterness if your trust is violated.

MAY 30

You have a quick temper and are inclined toward dominating and dictating your ideas, desires, and opinions. You are sorry immediately when you have let your emotions get beyond control. You like good literature and the pleasure of associating with interesting and witty people.

MAY 31

You are artistic and like to dress well and make your home different and attractive. You are sociable, congenial, and like club life. You are fond of children and take a great deal of interest in the proper upbringing of your own.

MEMORANDA

JUNE

BIRTHSTONE—Pearl: Health
FLOWER—Rose
COLORS—Light Blue and White

June 1 to June 22 _____ Gemini
      Governed by Mercury
      Mate in Libra, Aquarius, or Gemini

June 23 to June 30 _____ Cancer
      Governed by the Moon
      Women mate in Pisces or Cancer
      Men mate in Pisces, Virgo, or Libra

JUNE 1

You have a bright and cheerful disposition. Your confidence in whatever you are undertaking is steadfast, and no one can discourage you, but if failure comes, your disappointment is keen. You are fond of music and reading. Your home is very dear to you, and you derive your greatest happiness from it.

JUNE 2

You have considerable literary ability and should develop it. You are impulsive, and your mind is intuitive and imaginative, rather than analytical. You are devoted to your home and family and will make a happy and pleasant home life of your own.

JUNE 3

The easiest path is the one you pursue. You are independent and have originality and a fair amount of ambition, but your love of ease and comfort deters you from the greater success of which you are capable. You are moody and often depressed. You love deeply and faithfully.

JUNE 4

You are exceedingly optimistic, even in the face of disaster. You are bright, witty and good natured, are thorough in your work, and do it with ease and enthusiasm. You have many friends and will make a happy marriage and command a strong and devoted love.

JUNE 5

You have very definite emotions; you love deeply and hate intensely. You play wholeheartedly and work with enthusiasm and concentration. You make and act on all decisions quickly. Usually kind and thoughtful, you sometimes speak brusquely and harshly under provocation.

JUNE 6

Energetic, compelling, a clear thinker, shrewd, and cautious, you are successful in almost all you undertake, unless your better judgment yields to an outside influence. You are sympathetic, loving, and understanding, and your home is very dear to you.

JUNE 7

You are impulsive, act quickly, and are easily discouraged, although you are a loyal friend and always anxious to help those in need. You are sympathetic and sensitive, and you love with your whole heart and suffer deeply if love is not returned to you with an equal strength.

JUNE 8

You are just and ambitious, like to read and travel, and are apt in forming new friendships. You are sometimes stubborn in your viewpoints, and you are exacting and plan and do all things with meticulous detail.

JUNE 9

You are charming and gracious and have a sweet disposition. You have a keen and active mind, are determined and concentrated in your work, and have a goodly amount of executive ability. You are a good entertainer and are popular in your own social circle.

JUNE 10

You are ambitious and venturesome and apt to rush into things. You are led with better results than if you were driven. You are conscientious and sincere in everything. You are capable of a strong and lasting love.

JUNE 11

You are an omnivorous reader, an intellectual thinker, and a sparkling conversationalist. Your judgment is good and you never act in haste. You have great personal pride, like to dress well, and have a sincere devotion for your family. You form and keep friendships easily and will be very happy.

JUNE 12

With your musical and artistic ability, you seek the friendship and society of those who appreciate and love these things. You are both admired and popular among your friends and associates. You have an affectionate nature and, when you marry, you are assured of complete happiness and contentment.

JUNE 13

You are impulsive, energetic, and argumentative and put more faith in your intuition than in your judgment. You are a good and loyal friend and a bad enemy. You are demonstrative in love, and your happiness in love depends on receiving as much as you give.

JUNE 14

You are generous, kind, and considerate. You are capable and reliable and have a keen, active mind, and you are diplomatic and aggressive. You make friends easily and are fortunate in having a congenial trend of common interests. You are usually happy and contented but require love to keep your happiness.

JUNE 15

You are quick witted, intellectual, serious, and diligent in all you do. You enjoy reading and have considerable critical ability. You have many friends and are popular among them. Your home is dear to you, and you will have a happy married life.

JUNE 16

Although changeable and restless, you do tasks faithfully and to your best ability, even though they might be irksome to you. You are led by your inward desires rather than by outside influences. You are affectionate and sincere, and you will not fall in love at first sight. You are sometimes obstinate and like to have your own way.

JUNE 17

You have a blithe, happy-go-lucky manner and are friendly and entertaining. You are artistic, idealistic, and sometimes impractical, as well as sympathetic, loving, and devoted to your home life. You enjoy travel and its educational value and are eager to improve yourself. You will have a pleasant home life.

JUNE 18

Practice self-confidence. You have ability, but, through your modesty and diffidence, you allow others with less ability to carry on at your expense. Your charming personality makes many friends like and respect you. You are the clinging type and will choose the complement of your nature, a masterful and compelling mate.

JUNE 19

Sensitive, retiring, sympathetic, and loving, you yield
to another's opinion rather than take a definite stand
for yourself, even though you have strong convictions of
your own. You are affectionate but have few intimates.
To be happy, you need love and a sharing of your life and
happiness.

JUNE 20

You have originality and some executive ability and
mechanical skill. You are serious, and you think deeply and
keep your own counsel in your personal affairs. You are
generous and considerate and take much interest in affairs
other than those in your regular routine. You have many real
friends and love your home and all family ties.

JUNE 21

You are mechanically inclined, and it shows in your choice of work and recreations. You have a pleasant and congenial disposition and are kindly, slow to anger, and quick to forgive and forget. You enjoy and seek the society of witty people and are quick and amusing in repartee. You will marry young and be very happy.

JUNE 22

You are sensitive, retiring, interested in the lovelier things, an ardent reader, and an amusing and interesting conversationalist. You love to travel and will do so, and you enjoy outdoor sports. You will be a loving parent and a devoted mate.

JUNE 23

You are enthusiastic in all you do, as well as imaginative
and fun loving, and you are domestic and take great pride in
making your home attractive and pleasant. You are loving
and kind and will make a happy marriage.

JUNE 24

You are quick and have a good, clear-thinking mind, although
you are sometimes unintentionally brusque in your speech.
You have strong determination and the conviction of your
ideas. You make friends and hold them. The love you will
compel will be strong and steadfast.

JUNE 25

You are blithe and happy and have many loyal friends who always help you out when you are in difficulty. Be more cautious and give due consideration to what you are going to do; you are apt to rush into things too quickly. You are charitable and tolerant in your judgment and capable of strong and sincere love.

JUNE 26

You are witty, amusing, genial, and your friends like and admire you. You have a brilliant mind and like to read, and you enjoy mingling with intellectual people. You will be unusually happy in your married life.

JUNE 27

Your devotion to your life partner is demonstrative and supreme. Your home life is pointed out as ideal. You are kind, generous, and loving, and, with your high ideals and ambition, you will generally succeed.

JUNE 28

You are blithe, poetic, and sometimes volatile. You love with ardor and sincerity, and, though you are changeable in other things, your love is steadfast. You are a true and loyal friend, and you make many willing sacrifices in behalf of others you love.

JUNE 29

You have an alert mind, and you think deeply. You are forceful and determined and have good, sound judgment. You are uncommunicative and have a quick and violent temper, but love with the same impulsiveness and intensity. To be completely happy, you need someone on whom you can lavish your affections.

JUNE 30

You are self-reliant and confident in your abilities. You are very interested in and sensitive to art and artistic surroundings. You acquire knowledge easily and can impart it to others, which is a rare gift, and you would make an excellent teacher.

JULY

BIRTHSTONE—Ruby: Contented Mind
FLOWER—Larkspur
COLORS—Green and Russet

July 1 to July 22 _____ Cancer
    Governed by the Moon
    Women mate in Pisces or Cancer
    Men mate in Pisces, Virgo, or Libra

July 23 to July 31 _____ Leo
    Governed by the Sun
    Women mate in Aries
    Men mate in Aries or Sagittarius

JULY 1

You are artistic, poetic, and fond of music, and you like to travel. You are neat in your dress and your work, you adapt yourself easily, and you are friendly and popular in your own circle. You will be successful through your strong will and ambition for leadership. Your family is dear to you.

JULY 2

You are scrupulously honest and upright and have pride and a tender conscience. You have a lot of originality and an active mind. You are kindly toward your family and very popular with your friends.

JULY 3

You are a convincing talker, studious, and rather opinionated and independent, but, on the other hand, you are self-contained, sympathetic, and kindly. You are more popular with the opposite sex than with your own. You like travel and get a great deal of fun out of life. You are sincere in your affections.

JULY 4

Although you are not at all demonstrative, you love deeply and wholeheartedly. You have a strong and overpowering personality and generally rule by force of will. Cautious and careful, you select your words with care and mean what you say. You make many friends and few enemies.

JULY 5

You profit more by experience than by foresight. You are persevering and faithful, and adversity does not deter your ambition or change your plan of work. You are friendly and like attention; in love, you are steadfast and devoted.

JULY 6

You are serious in everything you do: love, work, or recreation. You are a great reader, a profound thinker, and an ardent student, and you make the most of your abilities. You enjoy culture and refinement, and whatever you undertake is done to the best of your ability.

JULY 7

You are usually kind, generous, and sympathetic. You are quick, energetic, and alert and can generally succeed in getting your own way. You have an interesting personality and will be happily married.

JULY 8

You are interested in art and music, but you have more talent in the latter, which should be developed. You are quick, energetic, and alert and can generally succeed in getting what you want by your shrewd scheming. You have an interesting personality and will be happily married.

JULY 9

You are ambitious and conscientious in your work and you are calculating rather than enthusiastic. You are original and resourceful in your methods. You have good judgment, and your deductions are generally correct. You are fond of children and your home, and you do all in your power to make your domestic life happy.

JULY 10

Cultivate and acquire more self-confidence. You are conscientious and trustworthy in carrying out another's plans but hesitant and indeterminate in your own. You are kind, gentle, sympathetic, and understanding, and you love deeply.

JULY 11

Yours is a sunny, radiant disposition, and your charming personality wins you many true and loyal friendships. You have good judgment and self-control. You like pleasant surroundings and create a pleasant atmosphere in the most unpromising environment. You will have a sincere love, and your home life will be ideal.

JULY 12

You are blessed with unlimited ability. You would find success in anything you undertook if you applied all your efforts faithfully. You are upright and have fastidious tastes and sound judgment; you are dependable and loving and enjoy and seek a harmonious life with pleasant surroundings.

JULY 13

You are a clear thinker. You make decisions quickly and act impulsively. You are energetic and aggressive; an omnivorous reader, you are ambitious for intellectual betterment. You like to travel and will do so. You are demonstrative and constant in your love.

JULY 14

With your sincerity and straightforwardness, you cannot tolerate or understand anything different in others. You are optimistic, generous, confiding, and idealistic and would suffer terribly if an ideal were shattered. Your love is pure, and, to be happy, you must have the understanding of your partner.

JULY 15

Inclined toward fretting and worrying, you are generally pleasant, loving, and kind. You are witty and fond of fun. You are blessed with intuitive and psychic powers, keen perception, and a vivid imagination. You will marry young and be happy in the love of a congenial mate.

JULY 16

You are positive and almost stubborn. Your very definite ideas of right and wrong are emphatic, and you cannot tolerate the slightest deviation from them in others. In your passion for correctness, you endeavor to have your friends follow your own ideals.

JULY 17

You are self-reliant, resourceful, and very understanding. You spend much time and thought in making your home artistic and attractive. You enjoy entertaining and are an interesting and brilliant conversationalist. By your kindly manner, you will create a happy and pleasant home life.

JULY 18

Yours is a fastidious nature. You like to dress well and appear at your best always. You are original and studious, and you like and appreciate art. Your disposition is generally sweet, and, although you sometimes lose your temper, you quickly recover it. You are affectionate and loving, and your home is very dear to you.

JULY 19

You have a vivid imagination, great ambition, and boundless energy. You like to travel, and you love the out-of-doors. In love, you are sincere and wholehearted and require the same in return.

JULY 20

You are shrewd, honest, studious, and conscientious in your work. You are rather outspoken and straightforward but tactful. You like society and are very popular in your own circle. You will be happily married and will make a pleasant and attractive home.

JULY 21

You are self-sufficient and intellectual and like to assume a leading role. You are adventurous and like to travel, and you are very healthy and robust and participate in many sports. You have the power and courage of your convictions and will yield a point only when the opposing viewpoint is proven to you.

JULY 22

You have a happy and even disposition and should marry young, preferably to someone with an emotional complement to your quiet temperament. You are versatile and resourceful and have a keen, penetrating mind. You are friendly, you appreciate the good in others, and you are fair and generous in every way.

JULY 23

You are energetic, vivacious, and rather talkative, and you are very fond of gaiety and social life and like to have an active part in anything you undertake. You are not demonstrative in your love and require affection and understanding from your mate.

JULY 24

Everything you do is done with intensity. You are emotional, quick tempered, and positive in your ideas. Practice self-control! You are a fond parent, and kind and sympathetic, and you love your family.

JULY 25

You have a magnetic personality, you make friends easily, and you are popular with everyone. You have good business sense and executive ability and are unusually fortunate in all your dealings. You are openhearted and sincere, and you love with a deep and strong devotion.

JULY 26

You are capable and dependable, although you are rather domineering. You are fond of good literature, and you are a fluent and intelligent talker and an amusing entertainer. You prefer the company of the opposite sex. Marry young and your home life will be congenial and happy.

JULY 27

You concentrate your earnest efforts on all your undertakings and, with your ambitions and determination, you are capable of great success and happiness. You are vivacious and lovable and your friends are true and loyal to you. You love with your whole heart and need sincere and constant love in return.

JULY 28

You have a keen, alert, and active mind. You are energetic and, when working under any strain, you are nervous and somewhat petulant, although charming and happy when your mind is free. You enjoy culture and refinement, love children, and will be happy in your own home.

JULY 29

You have a keen sense of humor and a quick wit, and you like excitement and gaiety and are generally well-liked. You are energetic, idealistic, imaginative, fond of art and music, altruistic, and generous to a fault. You are affectionate and domestic.

JULY 30

You have definite likes and dislikes. You make few friends, but those few are real and loyal to you. You are ambitious, energetic, and persevering, and you adapt yourself readily to every necessity. You are demonstrative in your great love of your family. Your interests center around your home and dear ones.

JULY 31

You are cautious, careful, and a good planner, and you have a fair amount of executive ability. Because of your keen foresight and good judgment, many seek your advice and profit by it. You are frank and honest in your judgment of others. Take care in the selection of your mate and do not marry in haste.

MEMORANDA

AUGUST

BIRTHSTONE—Sardonyx: Conjugal Felicity
FLOWER—Gladioli
COLORS—Orange and Red

August 1 to August 23 _____ Leo
    Governed by the Sun
    Women mate in Aries
    Men mate in Aries or Sagittarius

August 24 to August 31 _____ Virgo
    Governed by Mercury
    Mate in Virgo, Libra, or Sagittarius

AUGUST 1

You have intuitive powers and somewhat fastidious tastes, and you are bold even to the point of being foolhardy. You have perseverance and through it overcome many difficulties. You are fond of outdoor sports and travel. You are gentle, affectionate, and fond of children, and you love your home and family.

AUGUST 2

You are apt in handling details, have business ability, are aggressive, and adapt yourself readily to the job at hand. You are buoyant, happy, and sincere, and you like the company of cultured and refined people. You are a good conversationalist, fond of music and art. Choose a congenial mate, and you will be happy.

AUGUST 3

You are uncommunicative and independent and have great perseverance. In a quiet, modest way, you carry out your plans, relying on your own good judgment. You are affectionate and demonstrative and require a steadfast love from your mate.

AUGUST 4

Although you are positive, somewhat opinionated, willful, shrewd, and intellectual, you are just and sincere and do many kind and noble deeds unknown to others. You are friendly and have many fine friendships. Your home and family ties are dear to you.

AUGUST 5

You have good judgment, are quick witted, capable and observing, and always appear at your best. You have an artistic temperament, and you are neat and rather fastidious. You are an amusing and clever entertainer and popular among your friends. You are not demonstrative in your love, but your home life is ideal.

AUGUST 6

Marry young! Select a mate who is positive and self-assertive. You are emotional and sometimes tempestuous, and you are ambitious for social and intellectual improvement. You are an extensive reader, you talk fluently, and you take a great deal of interest in social and club life.

AUGUST 7

You have a nice sense of humor and can appreciate a joke even at your own expense. Although proud and somewhat positive, you have a strong, winning personality. You are energetic and original and are most happy when solving some problem. You are not demonstrative, but you are capable of a deep and true love.

AUGUST 8

You have a very sensitive, intuitive nature with almost psychic powers. You have fine executive ability and are particularly apt in handling people. Your personal desires and wishes are given preference in your family. You are affectionate and sincere.

AUGUST 9

You have definite likes and dislikes, but your love is sincere and strong. Your somewhat domineering, opinionated, and moody nature makes you seem ungracious under opposition. You are very honest and just and are unsympathetic to the injustice of others. Art, literature, and music are your great interests.

AUGUST 10

You are generous and must take care that you do not overlook your own interests. You have great executive ability, good judgment, and take a prominent part in everything. You are a good talker and convincing in an argument. Although you have many outside interests, you make your home life happy and pleasant.

AUGUST 11

You have positive ideas and opinions but are sometimes diffident. You have determination, perseverance, and energy, and you are fond of sports and pleasures. You will not fall in love at first sight, but when you do love, you will do so thoroughly and with absolute devotion.

AUGUST 12

With more than ordinary ability, you have self-confidence and ambition and work and plan in a methodical manner. You speak quickly sometimes but do not intentionally hurt others. You love travel and good times and want your family and loved ones to share all your pleasures. You are affectionate and loving.

AUGUST 13

You are ambitious, have high ideals, determination, and energy, are very trustworthy, and strive to excel in whatever you undertake. You are sentimental and loyal, and you love your family above everything else. You are loved by all because of your sympathy and generosity.

AUGUST 14

You have an alert and keen mind and good executive ability. You enjoy cultured and refined people. You are happy and optimistic and have a pleasant disposition. You do not care for the light or frivolous and you love your home and, in love, you are true and sincere.

AUGUST 15

Although aggressive, versatile, and sometimes arbitrary, you are determined and not easily discouraged in the face of failure; you usually accomplish your purpose one way or another. You love children and your home and have many loyal friends.

AUGUST 16

You are systematic, conscientious in details, slow, and generally accurate. You will be a devoted parent, a loving mate, and a loyal friend; you are a general favorite with your friends and associates.

AUGUST 17

Cultivate and practice self-confidence! Although capable of great success, you are apt to keep in the background. You are fair-minded, generous, kind, and considerate, and you are affectionate but not demonstrative.

AUGUST 18

You are acquisitive and have a quizzical and philosophical turn of mind. You are courageous, positive in your ideas and tastes, resourceful, and intellectual. You enjoy good reading and strive to improve your mind and to acquire the friendship of well-educated people. You will marry young and be happy.

AUGUST 19

You are impulsive and quick tempered but not unreasonable.
You have confidence in your ability and are ambitious,
determined, observant, and systematic. You like to make
others happy, and you are capable of an undivided love and
devotion.

AUGUST 20

You are a leader among your friends and in business. Your
ideals are high, and you should let them lead you, for they
will take you far. You are jovial and vivacious and fond of
out-of-door sports and travel, and you are well liked by
both sexes.

AUGUST 21

With your magnetic and strong personality, you have great powers for good or evil; people instinctively follow your lead. You are critical, rather opinionated, aggressive, and adaptable, and your judgment is usually accurate. You enjoy music and strive to make your home pleasant and attractive.

AUGUST 22

You have a winsome and off-handedly humorous way of getting your own way. You are somewhat fastidious, have self-reliance, and are modest and amiable. You have the ability to make others see things your way, and you will compel a deep and tender love.

AUGUST 23

You are robust and vigorous, you excel in all outdoor sports, and are skillful in any athletic contest. You have a keenly alert and inquisitive mind and an abundance of energy. You are resourceful, kind, and you make close friends easily. You love your home dearly and will be very happy in marriage.

AUGUST 24

You are honest, just, generous, affectionate, and farsighted, and you have good judgment. You love music and have considerable talent for it. You are an amusing and interesting talker, and you are humorous and good company. You love your home and are solicitous for the happiness of your family and loved ones.

AUGUST 25

You have the characteristics of a leader; you are affable, diplomatic, and careful of appearances and seldom show any agitation on the surface. You are sincere and demonstrative in your love and bitter in your hatred. Pick a congenial mate and you will be very happy.

AUGUST 26

You are literary and artistic, versatile, and rather headstrong. You are admired by your friends for your dependability, coolness, and reserve. You take nothing for granted, and you will have a happy home and marriage.

AUGUST 27

You are studious, clever, and rather serious minded. You have a keen, intuitive judgment, and a touch of satirical humor, which, though never severe, your friends avoid having directed at them. You are kind and loving, and always generous to your enemy. You will choose a genial mate and be very contented.

AUGUST 28

You are slow and deliberate, orderly, systematic, and methodical; you give full consideration to all sides of a situation before entering into it. You accomplish whatever you undertake and are generally accurate in your judgment. You will find your mate under the sign of Virgo.

AUGUST 29

When you choose, you can be an amusing and entertaining talker. You are fond of music and art, enjoy intellectual recreation, and like the society of cultured people. You are somewhat serious, and the lighter things do not interest you. You have few close friendships.

AUGUST 30

You have great originality and always do the unusual. You have a magnetic temperament and are brusque in your speech, intuitive in judgment, and demonstrative in your love. Generous, considerate, and unselfish, you receive many confidences. Your home life is pleasant and harmonious.

AUGUST 31

You read extensively and assimilate information readily. You are forceful, energetic, and ambitious and have a liberal, general ability, which will bring you success in all you undertake. Your opinions are sought and respected. Marry early in life and you will be very happy.

MEMORANDA

SEPTEMBER

BIRTHSTONE—Sapphire: Love
FLOWER—Aster
COLOR—Brown

September 1 to September 23 _____ Virgo
      Governed by Mercury
      Mate in Virgo, Libra, or Sagittarius

September 24 to September 30   Libra
      Governed by Venus
      Mate in Libra, Virgo, or Aquarius

SEPTEMBER 1

You are extremely generous in thought and deed, kind, hearty, and robust. You have much sentiment and are loyal to your kindred. You sometimes speak abruptly but do not mean to be unkindly. You are demonstrative and affectionate in your love, and you will receive the same in return.

SEPTEMBER 2

Always the life of the party, you are witty, bright, friendly, a good conversationalist, and well liked. You have friends in several distinct circles and can adapt yourself to each one. You radiate vitality and are domestic and loyal, and you love with sincerity and strength.

SEPTEMBER 3

You are conservative in your judgment and your methods of execution. You have mechanical ability and are methodical, patient, observant, and versatile. You do not make friends or attachments hastily and will probably not marry young. Your love will be strong and lasting.

SEPTEMBER 4

You are quick, volatile, and tempestuous and carry a point by force of will. You have a keen, brilliant mind. You like to work things out alone and are sometimes impatient in your haste to get them done. You are a true and loyal friend.

SEPTEMBER 5

Cultivate your self-confidence and don't give way to moods so easily. You are impetuous, vivacious, sometimes unsteady in your judgment, and generally very interesting. You like society, excitement, and pleasures, but you are capable of seriousness if necessary. You are winsome and loving.

SEPTEMBER 6

You are very conservative, planning carefully and working slowly and faithfully, for you enjoy seeing a job well done. In spite of your strong will, you are sometimes led by others. Domestic, gracious, and sympathetic, your love is strong and true, and your home life is ideal.

SEPTEMBER 7

You have great executive ability and are authoritative, determined, persevering, and self-reliant. You should go far in your chosen field. You enjoy reading good books and like to travel. You have high aims and ideals and have the respect and esteem of your friends and associates.

SEPTEMBER 8

You are artistic and musical, have positive ideas, and like having your own way. You are discriminating and shrewd, a good student, a deep thinker and an interesting talker. Loving, faithful, and devoted to your family, you will probably not fall in love at first sight.

SEPTEMBER 9

Magnetic, intuitive, and with some latent psychic powers, you have many different interests and have a leading part whenever possible. You are apt to rush into things without determining the outcome and should be more discriminating in your judgment. You are loving, kind, and considerate.

SEPTEMBER 10

You are uncommunicative and do not like to be questioned about your own affairs or those of anyone else. You are ambitious and resourceful, as well as impulsive and emotional, and you are guided by your intuition. You love your home and family and are capable of a deep and fervent love.

SEPTEMBER 11

Conscientious and ambitious, you are thorough and capable in your work, as well as a good planner, and you are competent in executing your plans. You have a keen mind, good judgment, and are sincere and honest. You will be a loving mate and parent.

SEPTEMBER 12

You are methodical, thorough, faithful, and a good worker. You are generally quiet and reserved, and you possess a subtle and amusing sense of humor. When aroused, your temper is strong but short lived. You make your home pleasant and attractive and are demonstrative in your love.

SEPTEMBER 13

You are strong and robust and love all outdoor sports. You work and play with equal strength and strive to excel in whatever you do. You are amiable, gracious, and discreet, and you have the confidence of your associates. If you marry young, you will be very happy. You are loving and sympathetic.

SEPTEMBER 14

Learn to assert yourself and be more aggressive! You are self-reliant and ambitious but very modest; you could achieve much more if you let yourself do so. You are musical and literary, and you love with your whole heart.

SEPTEMBER 15

You are exceedingly honest and frank as well as determined and energetic, but you are apt to use your energy in the wrong direction. You are cheerful and witty, good company, and a general favorite. You love your family and are dearly loved by them.

SEPTEMBER 16

Your tastes are simple but excellent. You are domestic and require only pleasant and harmonious surroundings and one to love and be loved. Demonstrative, impulsive, and somewhat jealous, you are easy to please and should take care in choosing your mate.

SEPTEMBER 17

You consider both sides of a question before making any decision, because of your analytical turn of mind. Painstaking, reliable, and competent, you will be successful in whatever you do. You enjoy traveling and good literature, and you strive to better yourself. Your home life will be happy and contented.

SEPTEMBER 18

You are sometimes impetuous, diffident, or headstrong but usually kind, tender, and understanding. You are a good planner and use what you have to best advantage. You are genial and form friendships easily. You might fall in love at first sight and be very happy.

SEPTEMBER 19

Ambitious, energetic, and a hard, conscientious worker, you help those dear to you even at the cost of your physical well being. You are careful, accurate, discreet, and somewhat fastidious. You love music and literature and make an interesting conversationalist. You are loving and kind, and you will be contented.

SEPTEMBER 20

You are individual and original. You always do the unexpected in an unusual way. You are welcome in the society of cultured people. You like personal attention, and you can be led by someone who understands you.

SEPTEMBER 21

You are blessed with an indomitable spirit and will never acknowledge defeat. You are farsighted, resourceful, and intellectual and have good executive ability. You are affectionate, loyal, and fond of your home and friends.

SEPTEMBER 22

You are a dreamer, have a vivid imagination, and make elaborate plans that you never carry out. Cultivate self-reliance, perseverance, and foresight. You are loving and lovable as well as gentle and attractive, and you're a favorite among your friends and popular with everyone.

SEPTEMBER 23

You have an alert mind, learn quickly, are observant, and can readily do what you have seen others do. You lack originality, but you are careful and prudent. You are honest, considerate, and friendly. You enjoy attention, but, when it is not forthcoming, you do not complain.

SEPTEMBER 24

You have an abundance of natural ability, and, with your mind made up, you can accomplish much. You are impulsive, and your intuition is more apt to be correct than your careful reasoning. You like social life and have many enjoyable interests outside of your home.

SEPTEMBER 25

You are sincere, frank, and outspoken, though rather pliable and often perverse. Your tastes are fastidious; you like artistic surroundings, and spend much time in making your home pleasant and attractive. You are affectionate and demonstrative and will probably fall in love at first sight.

SEPTEMBER 26

You have much literary ability and read a great deal. You are ambitious, energetic, positive, and quite often stubborn. You will do much for love but will not be driven. You have many friends and are popular with them. Your love is deep and steadfast.

SEPTEMBER 27

You are conscientious about everything regardless of how small or menial it is. You like all of the arts and converse interestingly and intelligently on all. You are kind, generous, and sympathetic, and you will select a loving and understanding mate. Marry early in life!

SEPTEMBER 28

You are impulsive, emotional, and impatient and like to get results quickly. You have originality, are quite versatile, are quick to grasp a point and have good judgment. You have a keen sense of humor, are winsome and vivacious, and you are loving and demonstrative in your family. Your home life will be a happy one.

SEPTEMBER 29

You are courageous, and venturesome, energetic, and very strong willed. Through your strong personality, you are a leader among your friends. You like entertainments, and your friends are as gay and vivacious as you. You are lovable and have a deep affection for your family.

SEPTEMBER 30

You are studious, intellectual, and sincere and have great confidence in your own abilities. You play and work with the same vigor and strive to excel in both. You are not confiding, but you are the recipient of many confidences. You are kind and considerate in your home and are dearly loved by everyone.

OCTOBER

BIRTHSTONE—Opal: Hope
FLOWER—Calendula
COLORS—White and Yellow

October 1 to October 23_____ Libra
      Governed by Venus
      Mate in Libra, Virgo, or Aquarius

October 24 to October 31_____ Scorpio
      Governed by Mars
      Women mate in Virgo, Libra, or Scorpio
      Men mate in Cancer or Virgo

OCTOBER 1

You can adapt yourself to circumstances and environment, but you enjoy luxury and ease. You are sociable, magnetic, and a loyal friend, and you possess a happy disposition. You are idealistic and sensitive, and you like music and art and derive much pleasure from both. Do not marry in haste.

OCTOBER 2

You possess a sweet and kindly disposition and are well liked and admired; you have many friends and no enemies. You are fond of good literature and the higher type of entertainment. You are musical and you love children and your home. Your love is deep and constant, and you will have the undivided devotion of your mate.

OCTOBER 3

You have a keen mind and shrewd judgment and ability, and you are a great reader and a fluent talker. You have many true friendships, although you are not demonstrative or confiding. Your love is sincere and fervent. You are trustworthy and faithful and always discreet.

OCTOBER 4

You are vigorous and energetic, you love the out-of-doors and you enjoy any athletic sport. You have perseverance, farsightedness, and self-confidence and are meticulous in detail. You assume responsibility with ease and assurance and are generally successful. Your love is deep and strong.

OCTOBER 5

You are impulsive, changeable, and quick tempered, but you nevertheless have a strong character, forceful and compelling. You love nature, especially water sports. You are fortunate in having many dear friends and will have a very pleasant home life.

OCTOBER 6

You are energetic and competent, and you have considerable mechanical ability. You enter into things wholeheartedly and go through with your best efforts. You are respected and admired by all who know you. If you marry young, you will be happy and have an ideal married life.

OCTOBER 7

You are scrupulously honest, faithful to duty, and sincere, and you say just what you mean. Studious and intellectual, you are well informed, a clear, keen thinker, and a lucid talker. Do not marry young; you will judge people differently and by different standards as you grow older.

OCTOBER 8

Sincerity, frankness, and assurance are your chief characteristics. You are thorough in your work and usually succeed. You are quiet and reserved, and you do not like social life except in your own circle. With your friends, you are affable and entertaining.

OCTOBER 9

You have a clear and logical mind, as well as good judgment and confidence in your ability. You love children and like fun and amusement, as long as it does not interfere with your business. You are just and loving in your home, and you will find real happiness in your married life.

OCTOBER 10

You are bright and cheerful, witty, and a general favorite. Your carefree ways belie your strong character, good judgment, and capability in handling any situation. You have many real friends, love your home, and are affectionate and demonstrative in your love.

OCTOBER 11

Your mind is not an analytical one, but you are seldom misled by following your keen intuition. You are prudent, thorough, and accurate, as well as positive and assertive, and you like to have a prominent part in whatever you do. You are happiest in pleasant surroundings.

OCTOBER 12

You love, work, and play with enthusiasm and energy. You are proud and reserved as well as discreet in your associations, and you strive to attain high ideals. Choose a mate born under your own sign and you will be happy.

OCTOBER 13

You have the qualities of a great leader. You can grasp any situation quickly and accurately, and your judgment is good. You have an excellent memory, learn readily, and can command the attention and respect of others. You require a strong love and like attention.

OCTOBER 14

You are abrupt and impulsive and sometimes act without considering the consequences. You should marry someone who is easygoing and dependable to complement your nature. You are capable of a great and enduring love.

OCTOBER 15

You have very definite ideas and a matter-of-fact way about you. You lack imagination and enthusiasm. You are cautious, and conservative and have a goodly amount of business ability. You enjoy good literature, are fond of nature, and seek the society of cultured people. You have many friends and are devoted to your family.

OCTOBER 16

You are energetic and vigorous and have determination. You acknowledge defeat only when you have exhausted all your resources. You are kindly and sympathetic, your temper is not easily aroused, and you are quick to forgive. You will always be happy and contented.

OCTOBER 17

You are domestic, reliable, competent, and generally satisfied with yourself. You have definite likes and dislikes, and you are bright, witty, good-natured, and popular in your own circle. You should marry young.

OCTOBER 18

You are positive and determined and sometimes stubborn and impulsive. Do not give way to moods; you are capable and energetic and like to be a leader. You are very affectionate and demonstrative and require an understanding and constant love.

OCTOBER 19

You are sensitive and shy and should cultivate self-assurance, for you could accomplish much more if you were more aggressive. You love your home and pleasant surroundings and strive at all times to make others happy.

OCTOBER 20

You are of an easygoing, contented, and comfort-loving disposition, but these traits do not interfere with your faithfulness in duty. Capable and reliable, you are looked up to by all. You are fond of good literature, and you love your home life and are devoted to your family.

OCTOBER 21

You are a natural leader and have decided executive ability. You are also a leader in your social life and are responsible for many of the pleasant affairs your circle enjoys. You are charming and gracious and always appear to the best advantage, and you have many real friends and are loyal to them.

OCTOBER 22

You have a keen mind and shrewd judgment, as well as a strong will. You are robust and have unusual endurance under stress. You are bright, witty, and a good entertainer. Your life will be uneventful, but you will have the steadfast love of your mate.

OCTOBER 23

You are kind and affectionate and have an amiable disposition. You are gracious and self-contained, and you are a fluent talker and an extensive reader. You have musical ability and should develop it. Marry young and choose a congenial mate, one who will encourage your talents.

OCTOBER 24

You are persevering and determined and sometimes quite obstinate. Your determination of purpose brings you much success. You are a loyal friend and a bitter enemy. You are better liked by the opposite sex. Your love will not be a smooth path, but on the whole you will be happy.

OCTOBER 25

Cultivate perseverance! You lose interest in what you are doing before its completion. You have great nervous energy and like a change. You are proud and always strive to appear at your best. You possess a keen sense of humor and are a pleasant conversationalist and a great reader.

OCTOBER 26

Your home is your castle, and there are few things outside of it that interest you. You are intellectual, conservative, and artistic, and you enjoy reading and have considerable literary ability. You have a magnetic personality, enjoy the admiration of your friends, and have no real enemies.

OCTOBER 27

You are emotional and tempestuous, and you lose your temper quickly, but, just as quickly, you regain control of yourself. You are inclined toward nervousness and like to keep busy all the time. You are affectionate, demonstrative, and impulsive in your love and require a steadfast love in return. You should marry young.

OCTOBER 28

You are generous, lighthearted, and optimistic, and you are fond of entertainment and amusement. You are artistic and musical and take a prominent part in the social life of your circle. Although you are not confiding yourself, others confide in you. You are dependable, trustworthy, and sweet-tempered. You will have a happy and quiet life.

OCTOBER 29

You are accurate, careful, and conservative, and you have great ability in carrying out details and act only after due consideration. You are a fairly good planner, but you are better in the execution of another's plans. Do not let things annoy you simply because they do not suit you. You are fond of children and enjoy the out-of-doors and all sports.

OCTOBER 30

Independent, sagacious, and self-confident, you possess good executive ability. Love will play the most prominent part in your life; you should choose someone congenial with your own tastes and marry young. You like your own way and are apt to be petulant under much opposition.

OCTOBER 31

You are kind and loving, sympathetic, and quite sensitive, and you are very popular and a comfortable person to have around. Although you are retiring and unassuming, you have good judgment, once you make up your mind. You have many friends.

MEMORANDA

NOVEMBER

BIRTHSTONE—Topaz: Fidelity
FLOWER—Chrysanthemum
COLORS—Dark Blue and Red

November 1 to November 22 _____ Scorpio
    Governed by Mars
    Women mate in Virgo, Libra, or Scorpio
    Men mate in Cancer or Virgo

November 23 to November 30 _____ Sagittarius
    Governed by Jupiter
    Mate in Leo, Aquarius, or Libra

NOVEMBER 1

You are a great reader and an interesting conversationalist, and you always appear at ease. You are adaptable to environment and circumstances, quick witted and capable, and trustworthy to the minutest detail. You are both loving and lovable and very fond of your home life, and you enjoy entertaining.

NOVEMBER 2

You are bold and ambitious, and you have high ideals. You are very positive in your ideas and make an enemy rather than make any compromise. You are critical and very relentless in your punishment of wrong. Your mate will have to be tactful and have great understanding to make your home happy.

NOVEMBER 3

Impulsive and subject to moods, you will love with strength
and ardor and demand the same from your mate. You love
travel and change of scene and can readily adapt yourself
to any environment. You are generous and kind. It gives you
a great deal of real pleasure to help others.

NOVEMBER 4

You are careful, conservative, exacting, and very capable in
the handling of details. You are trustworthy and dependable,
your confidence is sought by many, and you have the respect
of everyone. You are fond of children and love your home
and strive to make it happy and attractive.

NOVEMBER 5

You possess good executive ability, considerable originality, and a keen intuitive judgment. You are enthusiastic and optimistic; your love is demonstrative, and you are generous, kind, and sympathetic. You enjoy good literature and have considerable musical ability. You should marry early in life.

NOVEMBER 6

You lack self-confidence and decision. You do much better under the supervision and direction of others. You are tender and sympathetic and devoted to your family, and you should marry someone who will inspire you to aspire to your best.

NOVEMBER 7

Learn to restrain your impetuous nature; you are quick
tempered and jump to conclusions hastily. Your judgment
is good and usually right if you take time to give it due
consideration. You are a jovial, fun-loving person and are
popular among your acquaintances. Your love is apt to be
tempestuous.

NOVEMBER 8

You are determined, discreet, and conservative. Your tastes
are fastidious, and you like the comfort and ease of luxurious
surroundings. You are an ardent lover, have musical ability,
and are shrewd and resourceful, and few people can get the
better of you.

NOVEMBER 9

You have persistence and determination and never acknowledge defeat. You do not confide in others, but you like to work out your plans alone and in your own way. You have many friends and are well liked by all. Your home life will be contented and happy, and you will have the undivided devotion of your mate.

NOVEMBER 10

You like to lead and will not take a secondary position if you can possibly help it. You are very public spirited and quite philanthropic. You love travel, reading, and music. You should marry someone who is sympathetic toward your broad interests.

NOVEMBER 11

You are shrewd, determined, and argumentative and take a strong stand against opposition when you think you are in the right. You do not like to be driven, but for love you will do a great deal. You have many friends and are generally happy and entertaining.

NOVEMBER 12

A fine retentive memory and a good mind for details are your chief characteristics. You are amiable, magnetic, and intuitive, and you are a favorite among your friends and always welcome at social gatherings. You like to travel and to read about it. You will have a harmonious and happy life.

NOVEMBER 13

You are frank, honest, and outspoken. You like a change of environment but are not too unhappy if your desires are not gratified. You read a great deal, and you are a fluent talker and very entertaining. Your home life will be happy and contented if you marry young.

NOVEMBER 14

You judge hastily and lose your temper easily, although you do not give way to violent fits of passion. You do not harbor any resentment, and, although you are prone to speak hastily, you are sorry afterward. You are magnetic, and people follow you readily.

NOVEMBER 15

You are persevering, patient, and attentive to detail and have considerable originality. You are practical and not in the least subject to flattery. You are quiet and self-contained, and you enjoy the company of your own sex, like the out-of-doors, and are the favorite in your own circle.

NOVEMBER 16

You are intellectual, capable, and discerning, as well as fond of good literature, and you are a convincing and fluent talker. You have a deep and spiritual nature, are orthodox in your views, and spend little time in unknown fields. Your love is strong and deep, and you will receive a true devotion in return.

NOVEMBER 17

You have good judgment and are a careful manager and a shrewd manipulator. Your ideas are practical, and you consider all details before entering into any undertaking. You are affectionate, tender, and dependable. Your friends rely on your judgment and have absolute faith in you.

NOVEMBER 18

You are conscientious, ambitious, accurate, and just. You do not act hastily, but you are steady and reliable. You always finish whatever you undertake. You are both artistic and musical and have high ideals. You are jovial, hearty, and fun loving, and you will be happily married.

NOVEMBER 19

Your life is uneventful and runs in a smooth and orderly
manner. You are happy and contented, as well as honest and
affectionate. You are generally a very pleasant companion,
but when your personal comfort is threatened you are apt
to be a bit selfish. You are sociable and have many warm
friends.

NOVEMBER 20

You have positive opinions but are not argumentative. You
keep your own counsel and never violate a confidence. You
are trustworthy and reliable and have much latent ability.
Your friends are those who have interests similar to yours.
You should marry early in life.

NOVEMBER 21

You are somewhat sensitive but considerate of the feelings and opinions of others. You are prompt, dependable, able, and competent, and you are an ardent reader, a clear thinker, and an interesting and entertaining conversationalist. Your home is dear to you, and you are very fond of children.

NOVEMBER 22

You let the wrongs of others worry you and seem to feel it is up to you to correct them. You are serious and studious and enjoy only the highest type of literature. You are always careful of appearances and are generally cautious. Your love is strong and deep.

NOVEMBER 23

You are determined and venturesome even to the point of recklessness; you are so positive in your opinions that when you know a thing to be right, it is almost impossible to move you. People sometimes accuse you of being stubborn. You are just and honest and very exciting. You love with passion and vigor.

NOVEMBER 24

You are very conceited, have good self-control, and are ambitious and idealistic, but you lack perseverance and quite often fall short of attaining your goal. You are musical and artistic, steadfast in your love, loyal to your friends, and loving in your home.

NOVEMBER 25

Quiet and unassuming, you are very capable and possess good executive ability. You think logically, have good judgment, always keep your emotions under control, and are rarely enthusiastic. You love music, art, and travel and are quite adaptable. Your home is all-important to you.

NOVEMBER 26

You are kind, generous, upright, and capable of great self-sacrifice. You are a favorite among friends and dearly loved by your family. You have a strong, magnetic personality and many warm friends.

NOVEMBER 27

You are humorous and easygoing, an omnivorous reader, a careful student, and a clear thinker. You are aggressive and original. You make a good leader, both in society and business. You like to excel in what you do, either in sports or in any serious undertaking.

NOVEMBER 28

You are gentle, kind, and loving but sometimes domineering. You are independent and uncommunicative and have a good deal of self-confidence in your own ability. You should marry early in life; your love is strong, and you need love and devotion in return.

NOVEMBER 29

You would rather do things yourself than direct others in doing it. You are quick, impulsive, and very energetic, and you are shrewd and capable and have good intuitive judgment. You like the out-of-doors and travel and have many interests outside of your regular routine. You are loving and understanding.

NOVEMBER 30

You are conscientious and thorough in all you do and have the confidence and respect of your friends. You are positive, quick tempered, and impulsive, and you have a keen sense of humor, a clear mind, and good judgment. Marry early in life, and your home life will be happy and pleasant.

DECEMBER

BIRTHSTONE—Turquoise: Prosperity
FLOWER—Narcissus
COLORS—Indigo and Green

December 1 to December 22_____Sagittarius
Governed by Jupiter
Mate in Leo, Aquarius, or Libra

December 23 to December 31_____Capricorn
Governed by Saturn
Mate in Libra, Virgo, or Taurus

DECEMBER 1

You are self-confident, reliable, and determined, and you are rather quiet and reserved but fun loving. You have a keen and alert mind and much executive ability. You are gentle and affectionate in your home and always strive to add to the happiness of your loved ones.

DECEMBER 2

You are ambitious, persistent, and shrewd. You have high ideals and are unforgiving toward wrongdoing. You enjoy entertaining, love music and good literature, and strive to improve yourself. Although sometimes impractical and temperamental, you are loving and happy most of the time.

DECEMBER 3

You are idealistic and impatient and judge hastily. Although you plan many things, you tire quickly and drop them before completion. You have a clear, bright mind and are very adaptable. You are kind, affectionate, and charitable, and you have many real friendships.

DECEMBER 4

You are very confident of your ability, and justly so. You like to lead and are well liked by all who know you, although you make few intimate friends. Shrewd, capable, persevering, and energetic, you accomplish successfully all you undertake. You are loving, affectionate, and good-natured most of the time.

DECEMBER 5

You are scrupulously honest, sincere, and frank. Your quiet, unassuming manner makes you a general favorite and earns you many true friends. You like to dress well, are proud and careful of your appearance, and enjoy the out-of-doors. Choose a congenial mate and marry young, and you will be very happy.

DECEMBER 6

You are original, cautious, and accurate and have great determination, and it is very hard to move you once your mind is made up. You are a sincere and loyal friend, and you sacrifice much for friendship's sake. You love travel. In your home, you demand obedience and get it through love rather than by force.

DECEMBER 7

You have shrewd intuitive judgment and an abundance of energy. You take great pleasure in overcoming difficulties and carrying out your plans. You are ready to follow a good idea or plan, but you will not be driven. Your love is demonstrative, your home is dear to you, and your disposition is generally cheerful.

DECEMBER 8

You are an ardent reader, preferring the more serious type of literature. You enjoy sports and travel. You are bright, witty, and entertaining, and you are welcome at every social gathering. Your love is strong and ardent, and you will be loved in the same way.

DECEMBER 9

You are slightly inclined toward pessimism and should strive to curb this tendency. You have keen intuitive powers and quite frequently save yourself and friends from disaster through it. You are kind, somewhat sensitive, versatile, discreet, and eager to learn. You are loving and considerate in your home.

DECEMBER 10

You are positive, honest, and sincere, and you have considerable executive ability. You are somewhat excitable, imaginative, impetuous, energetic, and capable. You have a clear and just mind. Your home is very dear to you, and you are kind and very affectionate.

DECEMBER 11

You speak and act hastily but mean no harm. You are a great reader and a good and entertaining talker. Bright, witty, and vivacious, you are generally the life of the party. You love luxuries and pleasant surroundings and are sensitive to your environment. Your love is constant and demonstrative.

DECEMBER 12

You are honest, loving, persevering, and unyielding. You are sympathetic, kind, helpful and generous, self-confident, and you accomplish most of the things you undertake. Your happy-go-lucky manner makes you a favorite with everyone.

DECEMBER 13

You are bold, fearless, venturesome, and impetuous, and you make decisions quickly and act on them immediately. You have the respect and esteem of all, and your opinions are always desired and respected. You have many friends, and your home life will always be happy.

DECEMBER 14

You have a logical mind and hold firmly to your opinions and ideals. You are positive and aggressive, sometimes domineering, sarcastic, and critical. You are serious and studious, although somewhat vain, and you enjoy witty and intellectual society.

DECEMBER 15

You are reserved and unobtrusive, and, in your own quiet way, you accomplish a great deal. You have a retentive memory, learn readily, and impart your knowledge easily to others. You would make an excellent teacher. You are bright, witty, and very entertaining, as well as fond of fun and traveling.

DECEMBER 16

You are spiritualistic, idealistic, and somewhat religious, you are fond of music and art, and you are a good entertainer and enjoy society. You are sincere, honest, and frank, although you have discretion and much tact. You are a loyal friend and a bitter enemy. Your home life will always be happy and harmonious.

DECEMBER 17

You are quiet, reserved, imaginative, sometimes impractical, and subject to moods. To be happy, you require a deep and constant love. You are generally bright and happy and usually manage to get a reasonable amount of comfort. You have few intimate friends.

DECEMBER 18

You are strong-willed, self-confident, and aggressive, and you are apt to brush opposition aside. Your emotions are absolutely under control, and it is hard to tell your true feeling about anything. You are just and sincere. Your friends all like and admire you.

DECEMBER 19

You are ambitious, capable, and thrifty and make the most of what you have. You will be successful. You are artistic, always appear to good advantage, and endeavor to make your home more attractive. You are kind, loving, and genial and have hosts of friends.

DECEMBER 20

You are honest, trustworthy, constant, and patient. You are methodical and accurate in your work, as well as punctual in your appointments and fastidious in your dress. You are domestic, but enjoy many outside interests. You are very affectionate but not demonstrative.

DECEMBER 21

You are very optimistic, original in your ideas, determined, shrewd, and persevering, and you usually carry out your plans to successful completion. You have many real friends and few enemies. You are domestic, fond of children, demonstrative in your love, and generally cheerful.

DECEMBER 22

A keen sense of humor is your chief characteristic. You are generous, kindhearted, affectionate, and careful to never hurt another's feelings. You are sociable, vivacious, and energetic, as well as independent, and commanding. Through your efforts, you will have a happy home life.

DECEMBER 23

You are blessed with a keen insight. You are capable and have much ability, and you are generous in your judgment and always willing to help someone. You are alert, cautious, confident, and successful in all your undertakings. You have many proven friends. You will not fall in love at first sight.

DECEMBER 24

You are bold and energetic, and you possess intuitive powers and latent talents, which you should develop. Your love is ardent and constant. You should practice self-restraint and not let your passions get beyond your control.

DECEMBER 25

You are an ardent and assimilating reader, and you are observant and an interesting and fluent talker. You are honest, conscientious, methodical, and discreet at all times. You are a true and loyal friend and have a sincere devotion to your loved ones.

DECEMBER 26

Learn to rely on your own judgment; it is good and will bring you much success. You are entertaining, intelligent, and fun loving and have marked literary ability. You are farsighted, conservative, good company, and a strong lover, and you take a deep interest in your home.

DECEMBER 27

You are calm and collected, considerate of others, kindly, and optimistic. You are ambitious, aggressive, and determined; reverses and failure do not discourage you easily. You are affectionate and demonstrative. You are fond of children, and your home ties mean much to you.

DECEMBER 28

You are energetic, shrewd, and diplomatic, and you are courteous and obliging. You make friends easily and are generally well liked. You are sincere and frank and do not stoop to gain a point. You are gentle and patient in your home and endeavor to make it happy and pleasant.

DECEMBER 29

You are resourceful, original, and courageous, and you are competent in handling details and have considerable executive ability. You love good literature, music, and art, and you are an interesting and amusing entertainer. Your love is strong and constant.

DECEMBER 30

You are studious, intellectual, cautious, and discreet, and you have a keen and alert mind. You are considerate of others, shrewd, and honest, and you love travel and out-of-door sports. Your home is dear to you, and your love is strong and ardent.

DECEMBER 31

You are impulsive and emotional in the affairs of the heart and need love and devotion to make you happy and contented. You are thorough, practical, and observant, and you have many friends and are an amusing entertainer.

MEMORANDA

ISBN-13 978-0-8118-4783-4 ISBN-10 0-8118-4783-7
Design by Alethea Morrison
Typeset in Memphis and Neutra
Manufactured in China

Chronicle Books endeavors to use environmentally responsible suppliers and materials in its gift and stationery products.

Chronicle Books LLC
680 Second Street
San Francisco, CA 94107
www.chroniclebooks.com

20 19 18 17 16 15 14 13 12 11